The Efficient Professional Series

The How-To Guide for Generations at Work

How Americans of Every Age View the Workplace,
and How to Work Productively With Every Generation

Robby Slaughter

Publisher
Method Press / An Imprint of AccelaWork
6100 Keystone, Suite #254
Indianapolis, IN 46220

For further information, please visit www.accelawork.com or
call 1-888-200-9387.

The How-To Guide for Generations at Work

Cover design by AccelaWork
Photograph by Neustockimages. Used with permission courtesy of
iStockPhoto.com.

First Printing: 2013
Second Printing: 2019

For my parents,
whose love spans the generations.

Foreword

I HAVE BEEN WRITING AND SPEAKING on the subject of generations in the workplace since 2000. I first noticed generational differences as I started my career in the mid-70's, when I looked around my department and said to myself, "Work will be great when the 'old' employees finally retire." The "old" employees were anyone more than ten years my senior: the Silent Generation, born before the end of WWII.

The big joke is that "Silents" are not only still in the workforce more than 35 years later, but in many cases they are corporate officers and board members, as well as sales, accounting, or R&D professionals. And my generation, the Baby Boomers, seems intent on working well past age 65. That is no surprise since our core value is work. It was a luxury to have only two generations in the workplace. Today, there are four—and soon to be five—with whom we must not just deal, but communicate, include, motivate, and promote.

Robby Slaughter first caught my attention when he presented on social media in the workplace to a mixed generation audience. He very quickly got us out of our seats—and our generational groupings. He guided and encouraged conversation between strangers of different age cohorts. This is a skill that managers and non-managers alike can learn—and this book teaches.

The How-to Guide for Generations at Work addresses the daily assumptions, stereotypes, and miscommunications that interfere with manager-to-employee conversations, manager-to-manager collaborations, and department-to-department cooperation. In other words, this book addresses how to get things done in a multi-generational working world that will ever be thus.

If there are generational issues inside of organizations, surely the same issues exist between sales representatives and their customers. And every unaddressed mismatch costs time and money no matter which generations are misaligned in their communication.

The author points out early in the book that not only does each generation view the purpose of work differently, but each generation has its own agenda: to establish and advance its own ideas. It is with these two dichotomies in mind that he presses forward with three tools for the reader to use.

Whether you are responsible for assembling cross-functional teams, stimulating innovation across an organization, providing excellent customer service no matter the age of the customer or the customer service rep, or you just want your multi-generational team to communicate, you will find great value in the tools provided in this book.

For me, the main takeaway is that the crush of work cannot be allowed to get in the way of improving one-on-one communication. At the most competitive time in our working lives, we need collaboration among and between functions, levels, and even divisions, in our organizations. It starts with one person who is willing to use the right tools to improve communication so that each generation can be heard, appreciated and function more smoothly with all of the others.

We will never again have only two generations in the workplace, so it is critical to become "multi-lingual." Robby Slaughter has provided a roadmap for those among us who want to accomplish more at a lower personal cost.

- Nancy S. Ahlrichs, SPHR, CDE

Introduction: A Practical Guide

IT'S NEARLY A GUARANTEE. Nearly every day, you work directly with someone outside your own generation.

But what's more significant is the "generation gap." The conflict and confusion. The frustrations and the idiosyncrasies. You can't believe that someone with so much youthful energy (or so much wisdom and experience) would operate that way.

What's worse is when those negative feelings evolve into prejudice. That's why we think of startups as being full of twenty-somethings and blue chip companies as dominated by gray-hairs. We make assumptions about age and technology, about age and intelligence, about age and education. We remove dates from our resumes and dress outside of our own decade. We use the year people were born in the one way we've sworn never to use gender, religion, race, and more.

But in the most successful businesses and non-profit organizations, age is neither an asset nor a liability. You're not promoted due to length of service, but level of contribution. You're never ordered to make coffee because of your youth. In fact, in these companies, nobody orders you around—ever. Age is a non-issue.

Unfortunately, you probably don't work in one of these environments. It's likely you deal with inter-generational issues on a regular basis. Whether it comes from older people or younger people (or both), generational stress is impacting you at work.

And let's be honest. You may actually be the *cause* of some of those issues.

In the pages ahead, you're certain to learn something new about each of the different generations in the modern workforce. The chapters have stories that may sound familiar, and some that are likely coming in your future if you haven't experienced them yet.

Next, you'll learn one guiding principle that will transform your interactions with people decades older and younger than yourself. This book explains how that one philosophy will completely change your worldview regarding generations in the workplace.

And then *The How-To Guide for Generations at Work* gets into the details. You'll learn three straightforward tools for engaging your colleagues. And then you'll see how these tools are applied in multiple different real-world scenarios, with activities you can try on your own.

So what are you waiting for? It's time to dramatically improve your relationships with old and young at work. Let's get started!

About the Series

The Efficient Professional books explain *precisely how* to increase your personal productivity at work.

There a variety of resources available that are filled with business advice. But unlike many others, The Efficient Professional lists exactly what steps you should take and provides hard evidence as to why.

Furthermore, this series focuses both on what to do as well as what *not* to do. Often, knowing what to avoid is even more important than knowing what to embrace.

Each book in the series contains a core idea that drives every recommendation. That means you don't need to memorize a vast number of rules or tips. Instead, the reader can build new habits around a single, easy-to-remember mission statement.

This way, referring back to different chapters and sections can be done quickly. Just recall the key concept, and turn to the appropriate page.

Finally, The Efficient Professional series offers fresh perspectives and does not merely rehash common sense. If you're ready to catapult your personal productivity, pick up any book in the series.

More information at **efficientprofessional.com.**

About the Author

Robby Slaughter is a workflow and productivity expert. His consulting practice assists a wide variety of organizations, including Fortune 500 companies, regional non-profits, small businesses and individual entrepreneurs to help increase productivity, simplify workflow and optimize business processes.

Robby's particular focus is the use of stakeholder-driven business improvement through the lens of process mapping. Working with individuals and small teams, he facilitates discussions in which problems and opportunities are rapidly identified. The collaborative and visual nature of this approach has a profound impact on organizations, which frequently see dramatic and sustained productivity gains within a few weeks.

Although this consulting process does not primarily employ technology, a background in computing drives this scientific approach to improvement. After an extensive career in IT systems development, Robby realized that the principal challenges affecting individual workers are not technological in nature, but psychological. He discovered that to become more effective and efficient at work, we need to empower individuals with authority and responsibility. His consulting practice now focuses exclusively on assessing workflow challenges, helping stakeholders to design and develop new business processes, and implement systematic, people-centered changes throughout the organization.

Robby is a regular contributor to several local and national magazines and has over three hundred published articles. He has been interviewed by multiple national and international publications, including the *Wall Street Journal*. Robby is a nationally known speaker. He is also the author of several books, including *Failure: The Secret to Success*, *The Unbeatable Recipe for Networking Events*, *The How-To Guide for Generations at Work*, *The Battle For Your Email Inbox*, and *The New Science of Time Management*. More information about Robby is online at robbyslaughter.com.

Table of Contents

PART I

THE FACE OF THE AMERICAN WORKFORCE

Amongst democratic nations,
each generation is a new people.

– Alexis de Tocqueville

Chapter 1

We See Everything Differently

Every generation laughs at the old fashions,
but follows religiously the new.

– Henry David Thoreau

FOR A HANDS-ON, CRASH COURSE on generational theory in the professional world, there is no better place to go than the unemployment office.

Watch people waiting in lines, filling out forms, or sitting in classrooms. The way they move tells you the decade they entered the workforce. Their reactions to educational material—be it relief, defiance, indifference, or dismissal—tells you more about them than you would learn in a typical job interview.

That's because the conference room is a rarefied environment where we have practiced being the person we believe others want us to be. But out in the real world, our rough edges are more apparent. There's something in our experience (or lack thereof) that gives us quirks we cannot truly control.

In short, we are all different. But we do fall into strikingly consistent groups. These classifications are characterized by our generation.

This distinction is a major strength.

The statement that our individual generation is an asset should be no surprise. Most modern societies value diversity. America in particular was founded and populated by people who came from all over the world.

And while those differences fuel our engine of innovation, they are also the source of significant friction. Although we may not always want to admit it, we consider ourselves to be different from those who do not share our gender, our race, our religion, our upbringing, or our politics.

More often than not, we gravitate toward people who are like us rather than those who are different. At work, we cluster especially into ages. This is human nature. It's hard to resist.

Usually, however, what matters most about diversity are not the differences in appearance—but differences in perspective. Consider this tense conversation among four people at an early morning meeting:

Eileen: "The customer is breathing down our neck. We need to get this out the door by the end of the week, no matter what it takes."

Randy: "Our company has had a reputation for quality for nearly fifty years. If we can't deliver something we're proud of, we shouldn't deliver at all."

Myron: "I've got an idea for a shortcut that may help us meet our deadline. It's not perfect, but I think it's a good compromise."

Sara: "Whatever you guys need me to do, just let me know. I can stay late tonight and help out."

Everyone may work in the same organization on the same projects, but each person has their own point of view. We're one enormous world of professionals, but we all see things differently.

Our perspectives at work are built upon these foundations:

✓ **Individual Personality** – An employee doesn't just bring their keys and security badge to work: they also bring their temperament. People may prefer exploring new ideas or sticking to established practices. They may seek the company of others or like working alone. Some individuals are agreeable and others want healthy debate. And there are those who focus on small details and those who want to discuss the big picture.

✓ **Professional Experiences** – Everyone comes from somewhere. Experiences may come from past work at your current employer, at previous jobs, internships, and in volunteer roles. If you've been burned (or rewarded) in a particular situation, that memory provides crucial guidance for what you'll do next.

✓ **Perceived relationships** – All individuals hold beliefs about how they relate to others. They may feel subordinate or superior, friendly or distant, trusting or fearful, or any other number of emotions. Most importantly, *perception is reality*. A strong conviction about a colleague's *perceived* opinion has more bearing on a person's actions than the truth.

✓ **Current Conditions** – Everyone at your workplace is carrying recent information that informs their point of view. This may be stress or excitement in their personal lives, business knowledge that has not or cannot be shared with everyone, or data known by everyone in the department. If someone knows a storm is coming, that data impacts their beliefs.

✓ **Culture and Identity** – Our perspectives are defined in part by who we think we are. This includes association (or disassociation) with family, religion, organizations, country of origin, and race. We all have values and beliefs, most of which have been with us longer than we can remember. Our viewpoint is most fundamentally defined by what we think is right, and that comes from our sense of self.

Each of these elements shines into our work and personal lives through the lens of our generation. That's not to say that, for example, Baby Boomers are more extroverted on average. Rather, it's that Baby Boomers tend to have a different point of view than other generations do on the role of extroverts.

Everyone has a unique, individualized perspective based on their personality, experiences, beliefs about relationships, current life conditions, as well as culture and identity. It's human nature to see things differently.

And unfortunately, it is human nature to have trouble seeing anything from another person's point of view.

One way to better understand this element of our humanity is through a major discovery of modern social psychology. Here's some dialogue that illustrates the principle:

> Naomi: "I'm going to have to come in on the weekend, even with Franklin now using the online system to process requests."
>
> Jeff: "You mean the new guy? Well, he's got to be at least fifty five. I'm not surprised he's slow on the computer. What do you expect? "
>
> Naomi: "I expect slow progress from someone brand new. Were you any faster with our technology your first week on the job?"

Researchers call this the *fundamental attribution error.* When it comes to explaining social behavior, we tend to overestimate the role of characteristics and underestimate the role of circumstances.

That is, we're more likely to assign blame for mistakes as well as give credit for successes based on disposition and personality. This is a mistake: we should be looking at the particular situation as well.

In the case of the story, Jeff reveals his preconception about age and technical proficiency. Naomi reminds him that practically everyone is slow when they are first learning the system.

The fundamental attribution error happens everywhere. What's worse is that it tends to be self-serving. If *someone else* trips and falls, it's because they are clumsy. If *we* stumble, it's because the sidewalk is uneven.

At work, this leads to either pulling our colleague aside to tell them to watch where they are going, or pulling the maintenance crew aside to be reprimanded. Neither of these outcomes will be helpful.

This phenomenon works in reverse, too. Sometimes, we think the reason "everything goes wrong for us" is because we are incompetent. We assume anything that goes well is just dumb luck.

What does the fundamental attribution error have to do with generations at work? Some people will:

⊘ Incorrectly assume that experience always means competence, no matter what the task.

⊘ Think they have no value because they have only been working a few years.

⊘ Attempt to match people together on projects based on their generation.

⊘ Believe they will always struggle with technology because they are older.

Those associations are unfair and destructive. But the challenge of engaging multiple generations requires more than just understanding a little about our own psychology.

We need to know who we are working with.

That's the topic of Chapter 2.

Chapter 2

The Story of Generational Theory

We need to remember across generations that there is as much to learn as there is to teach.

– Gloria Steinem

SO WHAT EXACTLY ARE THE GENERATIONS? How are they defined and what can science tell us about them?

First, it's important to note that the study of generations is nothing new. A Cambridge graduate student named Kenneth John Freeman writes about the changing perspectives of ages in his dissertation:

> Children began to be the tyrants, not the slaves, of their households. They no longer rose from their seats when an elder entered the room; they contradicted their parents, chattered before company, gobbled up the dainties at table, and committed various offences…such as crossing their legs.

Freeman's essay was published in 1907. But he wasn't talking about kids of his time. He was summarizing complaints about shifting attitudes that came from the ancient Greeks.

There's an important difference, though, in reflections about people based on their age and those based upon the particular era in which they were born.

Social scientists use the word *cohort* to describe a grouping of people. A cohort of individuals aged 20-30 is not necessarily the same as a cohort of individuals born between 1983 and 1993.

As psychologist Simon Poss notes:

> The [traditional] assumption is that values, attitudes, beliefs, and inclinations are primarily a function of age and maturity rather than generation. Generational cohort theory diverges from this perspective, arguing that changes across generations are primarily a function of social events rather than biological processes.

Therefore, the theory of generations is that *what happened to your generation* is what makes you different.

So what are the variations in each generation?

Here's where we get into the meat of the problem. Virtually everything we hear about generational theory has been repackaged or synthesized in one series of wildly successful books. Authors William Strauss and Neil Howe present a riveting description of the different cohorts, complete with lists of traits, limitations, and predictions about each group.

There's considerable debate among researchers about the limits of this field. A piece in *The Chronicle of Higher Education* by Eric Hoover notes:

To accept generational thinking, one must find a way to swallow two large assumptions. That tens of millions of people, born over about 20 years, are fundamentally different from people of other age groups—and that those tens of millions of people are similar to each other in meaningful ways. This idea is the underpinning of [their] conclusion that each generation turns a historical corner, breaking sharply with the previous generation's traits and values.

That might seem discouraging. However, scientists *do* have reams of research that shows that the year you were born has as much influence on your thinking as the household you were born into.

However, Hoover is right that shifts in perspective that are based on changing culture and current events happen gradually over time.

Does that mean generational theory is worthless? Not in the least. As Professor Amanda Griener notes in the *Journal of Social Issues*:

It is not where the divisions are drawn that is important, but how individuals and societies interpret the boundaries and how these divisions may shape the processes and outcomes.

So while we might use terms like "The Greatest Generation" or "Baby Boomers" or even "Generation Y", what is most important is not the watershed years (a specific timespan) but our interpretations of ourselves and others.

This is the practical upshot of studying generations: it's not how we're different that matters—it's how we choose to engage each other.

If the writings of Strauss and Howe are so controversial, what can we say for certain about generations?

Researchers tend to agree in one area: generational theory is *descriptive* more than it is *prescriptive*.

A birth year indicates what a person has experienced and suggests how they might view the world, but it does not necessarily predict their behavior or their weaknesses. A generation may *describe* but it does not *prescribe*.

For example, a person born in 1930 experienced the Great Depression as a child. It's reasonable to suggest that they understand scarcity in a very personal way.

Likewise, a person born in 1945 grew up in during a period of tremendous and unparalleled economic expansion. They are more likely to have a mindset of abundance and willingness to use and discard objects.

However, these suggestions do not mean people from the depression era are cheap and those born in the Baby Boom are wasteful. Rather the observations provide a framework for discussion based on real history.

Strauss and Howe do get some things right. For example, they write extensively about how one generation influences the next.

Depending on your age, it's likely you remember wanting to rebel against your parents as a teenager. Your reaction to their generation was likely a major factor in your own generational identity.

But doesn't *every* adolescent want to rebel against their parents, at least a little? The hard figures show the phenomenon is sociological, not biological. Dr. Robert Epstein, the former Editor-in-Chief of *Psychology Today*, writes in *Scientific American*:

> There is clear evidence that any unique features that may exist in the brains of teens—to the limited extent that such features exist—are the result of social influences rather than the cause of teen turmoil.

Epstein goes on to explain how teen rebellion does not really seem to exist in pre-industrial societies. For example, he notes:

> [Teen] delinquency was not an issue among the [native] Inuit people of Victoria Island, Canada, for example, until TV arrived in 1980. By 1988 the Inuit had created their first permanent police station to try to cope with the new problem.

Not all up-and-coming generations react with defiance. In Strauss and Howe's *Millennials Rising: The Next Great Generation*, they point to data that shows the younger cohorts are more trusting of parents and authority than previous groups.

In fact, surveys report they are more likely to enjoy the same music!

Our reactions to previous and subsequent generations are crucially important to understanding ourselves. As Epstein shows, these responses arise from our social experiences, not our brain chemistry.

Since generational differences do not arise merely from brain chemistry, our strategy must change accordingly. For example: in the journal *Currents in Teaching and Learning*, Michael Wilson and Leslie Gerber provide the following suggestions for educators working with younger students:

> ...that instructors deliberately *over-estimate* the desire of students for clarity—and resist the temptation to regard those students as

somehow deficient in character for the fervency of such a desire.

…letting their collaborative skills surface by inviting student input into the design of assignment types, grading systems or rubrics, and teamwork activities.

…that this ethical issue [of grade inflation] be regularly discussed with the students themselves, rather than simply being covered by a note in the syllabus.

These particular recommendations illustrate key differences in perspective across each generation. If the newer generation tends toward clarity, collaboration, and dialogue, a straightforward change may be beneficial.

The same is possible in working with any generation on any task—not just teaching millennial college students.

In summary: each generational cohort sees other cohorts differently. Using this knowledge can help us communicate and interact more productively.

So what's the problem?

Where generational theory gets us into trouble is when we use it to stereotype. We place people into a box based on their age, the same way that people are judged based on their gender, their politics, or their race.

Furthermore, people spend a great deal of effort trying to live outside of their own generation. Individuals will change their dress, dye their hair, tweak their résumé or change their vocabulary to try and seem older or younger.

Studying the generations can describe how people are likely to think and feel. It can even help us guess what they might do in a given situation.

But the year someone is born cannot prescribe their limitations.

It can only tell us something about the world that they have seen and the perspective they may have.

That's all a generation truly is.

Chapter 3

Four Generations, 150 Million Perspectives

The nation is a community.
Community of individuals, community of generations.

– Aleksander Kwasniewski

As of March 2013, the government's Bureau of Labor Statistics (BLS) reports that there are approximately 155,028,000 people in the labor force.

That number, not surprisingly, has changed. There are more people working today in America than there ever have been. But that's mostly because the population continues to rise. And not only is the country getting bigger, but we're living longer.

The life expectancy in the US was only 47 in 1900. By 2010, the number had jumped to nearly 79.

With all those extra years, we're not just taking a longer retirement. We're also putting in more years at the office.

Data from the BLS shows that as recently as 1967, only 3% of people over the age of 75 were employed. But that number has more than doubled as of 2013.

Even the percentage of employed Americans aged 45-65 has increased from 65% to 73%. Today, more than one fifth of the American labor force is aged 55 and above.

All of these numbers show that if you're not currently working with someone outside your generation, you will be soon. Even if you don't change jobs, the company may hire someone surprisingly young or surprisingly old.

No matter what generation you identify with, the makeup of each age group probably surprised you.

So what *are* the lines that separate each generation?

Unfortunately, researchers don't agree on where to divide each cohort, or even the name to use for each one. For simplicity, this book defines them as follows:

Born 1926-1945	Silent Generation
Born 1946-1965	Baby Boomers
Born 1966-1980	GenXers
Born 1981-2000	Millennials

These divisions are far from perfect (one is even smaller than the others.) But generational theorists *do* tend to agree that there is no perfect grouping.

If you fall near one of the dividing lines, you may feel more closely identified with one generation than the other.

But no matter what year you were born, every person and every generation has a story.

That story begins in the middle of the Roaring Twenties.

The decades following The Great War were one of the most prosperous, innovative, and positive periods in America's history.

The economy boomed. Between 1920 and 1929, the gross domestic product (GDP) rose by nearly 50%. In that same time, US automobile production nearly tripled.

Technology changed lives. Throughout the course of the decade, Americans living in homes with electricity shot from 33% to 70% of the total population.

Women gained more prestige in society at a rapid pace, earning the right to vote in 1920, presenting the Equal Rights Amendment to Congress in 1923, and electing the first female state governor in 1925.

In 1927 alone, Babe Ruth set the home run record. Charles Lindbergh made the first solo transatlantic flight, and the first "talkie"—*The Jazz Singer*—hit movie theatres.

Everything was looking up. Until one day: October 29, 1929. Black Tuesday.

The crash of the stock market was the most visible event in a series of economic calamities that led to the Great Depression.

It's difficult to imagine the economy dropping to a standstill like it did during the 1930s. A third of all the nation's banks failed. In some cities, the unemployment rate hit 80%. A million family farms were lost. Nine million savings accounts were virtually wiped out.

For the first time in generations, more people were leaving for other countries than were immigrating to the US.

Time passed, but the recovery was still slow. Even when the nation began to contribute to the war effort, the American culture was still one of shortages and conservation. In 1943, victory gardens produced 40% of the fresh vegetables in the country. Communities organized scrap and salvage drives. Propaganda posters encouraged car-sharing and limiting energy use.

A popular motto from the era summarizes the time:

Use it up.	Wear it out.
Make it do.	Or do without.

Children born between 1925 and 1945 were characterized in the November 5, 1951 cover story of *Time* magazine:

> Youth today is waiting for the hand of fate to fall on its shoulders, meanwhile working fairly hard and saying almost nothing. The most startling fact about the younger generation is its silence. ... It does not issue manifestos, make speeches or carry posters. It has been called the "Silent Generation."

If the children of the Silent Generation started their life dominated by scarcity, the Baby Boomers grew up in a world of abundance.

The Second World War destroyed the economy of virtually every major world power—except for the United States. When soldiers returned home many immediately returned to the workforce and started families. Others worked on themselves: the G.I. Bill provided loan guarantees, jobseeker assistance, and unemployment pay, as well as education benefits.

By 1947, veterans made up half of the total of U.S. college enrollment.

By the end of the 1950s, the nation's economy had grown by 37%. Unemployment bottomed out at 4.5%.

This was a decade of consumerism, but also one filled with the rumblings of social change. In 1954, the Supreme Court ruled segregation illegal. In 1955, a seamstress named Rosa Parks refused to give up her seat and move to the back of the bus. In 1956, Elvis Presley shocked one generation and rocked another by gyrating on live TV. And in 1957, a Soviet *sputnik* appeared in the skies above.

Some call 1960s the decade of discontent. The Berlin Wall was built in 1961, *Silent Spring*—the book that launched the environmental movement—was published in 1962.

And in 1963: the feminist movement leapt forward with the release of *The Feminine Mystique.* The national dialogue on equal rights culminated in the March on Washington and the "I Have a Dream Speech" by Dr. Martin Luther King, Jr.

In November of that year, John F. Kennedy was assassinated.

Between 1945 and 1964, 76 million American children were born. They came of age in a rapidly changing world, with shifting values and rapid advances in communication.

Many were raised in a new middle class. They had unprecedented access to capital, education, and opportunity.

This is a competitive but compassionate generation. They created the modern perspective on work.

And now, they are leaving behind their legacy. As of 2010, nearly 7,000 Baby Boomers hit retirement age daily.

The echo of the Boom reverberates to this day.

Children who came of age in the fifteen years following 1965 were raised in a period of renewed social consciousness. In 1967, Thurgood Marshall became the first African-American Supreme Court Justice. In 1969, astronauts first set foot on the moon. That was also the year *Sesame Street* first aired on television.

On April 22, 1970, over twenty million Americans participated in the first Earth Day rallies in every major city in the country. By the end of the year, Congress had created the Environmental Protection Agency and passed the Clean Air Act. Within the next few years, lawmakers enacted several other regulations designed to protect natural resources, including the Endangered Species Act.

Technology changed during this period at an even faster rate than before. Children raised between 1965-1980 saw the first pocket calculators and the first home computers.

The Voyager missions, launched in 1977, showed that mankind's reach was not just to the moon, but to the planets and beyond.

This is a generation raised on inclusion and seeking consensus, one which believed technology had the power not just to make nations stronger, but to make the world smaller.

This is the generation of choice, where anyone could pursue any career regardless of their gender, and anyone could choose family, career, or both—as they desired.

Photographer Robert Capa coined the term, but it was not popularized until much later:

> We named this unknown generation, The Generation X, and even in our first enthusiasm we realized that we had something far bigger than our talents and pockets could cope with.

❖ ❖ ❖ ❖ ❖

Children born between 1980 and 2000 are called *Millennials*, so named because of their connection to the end of the millennium.

This generation also experienced major social and political events. The 1980s and 1990s saw the collapse of the Berlin Wall, the Soviet Union, and Apartheid in South Africa.

These American children saw women in space, in the Supreme Court, as Secretary of State, and as a major party candidate for Vice President. By 1986, half of all college graduates were women.

But perhaps the most significant changes in this time were those in technology.

If the Boomers grew up with public technology and GenXers grew up with personal technology, the Millennials are those born into a world of social technology.

The first online tools for social exploration, the Bulletin Board Systems, came to life in the early 1980s.

Each BBS was operated independently using slow dial-up connections. In the twenty years of the Millennial generation, over 100,000 BBSes supported millions of users.

The BBS culture was soon to be replaced by a widely accessible global network. In 1985, there were less than 20,000 Internet users. That number shot to 28 million people as of 1995, and by December of 2000, the worldwide online population exceeded 430 million individuals.

Millennials grew up with access to email and instant messaging. Many joined MySpace and Facebook as teenagers.

As of the year 2000, 5% of 13-to-17 year olds had cellphones. By 2005, that number ballooned to 50%.

In *Millennials Rising*, Strauss and Howe write:

> The Millennial Generation will entirely recast the image of youth from downbeat and alienated to upbeat and engaged—with potentially seismic consequences for America.

They are now entering the workforce. Some are even taking on management roles.

And even more importantly, this is a generation of fearless entrepreneurs. In 2010—the year that the average

Millennial reached age 20—the number of new businesses created reached a 14-year high.

They are the youngest generation at work. And the way they work is fast-paced, highly collaborative, and affirmation-seeking.

The Millennials are a generation like none other.

These are the four generations in today's businesses. What next?

Certainly, every cohort is different. The challenge is not in recognizing there are variations. Instead, it's in working to understand this diversity in a way that helps progress happen on the job.

There is a way to bring ages together. That unifying principle is the reason we do what we do.

The secret to generations lies in knowing their purpose. If we know what makes them tick, we can motivate, communicate, and collaborate effectively.

That's the why it's time to ask *why*. It's time to ask *why* each generation goes to work.

Chapter 4

The Purpose of Work

Let us make future generations remember us as proud ancestors just as, today, we remember our forefathers.

– Roh Moo-hyun

WHAT EXACTLY is the purpose of work?

It might seem strange to ask this question. After all, doesn't everyone know why we work?

The answer is different depending on who you are. Some people work to support their families. Others work because they enjoy certain technical and physical tasks. Some like working because of their coworkers. And some people are just in it for the money.

There's no one right reason to work. We are all motivated by different factors. And it's easy enough to associate these with different generations.

For example, the Silent Generation grew up in a period of tremendous economic scarcity. So if people from this era are likely to say anything, it's to state they are thankful to have a job at all.

Boomers, on the other hand, probably have neither an innate sense of humility nor an innate sense of entitlement when it comes to working. Given the economic climate of competition and opportunity, they are most likely to work because they want to get ahead.

The next generation seems to interpret work as an obstacle to family. In a 2002 study by Catalyst, 59% of GenXers indicated a desire to telecommute. The survey reported 79% of women and 68% of men sought a flexible work schedule to spend more time with children. Generation X believes that work is a mechanism to support their personal life, but should not interfere with their interests or their families.

For Millennials, however, the most common purpose of work is about fulfilling a vision. That means they are interested in the entire role of the company within the ecosystem of customers, partners, vendors, and the local community. This generation goes to work because the organization's values align with their own.

Although each of these explanations might be appealing, none of them address the fundamental purpose of work itself.

Work is *not* about gratitude, competition, sustenance or a sense of identity. Rather, **the purpose of work is to be productive.**

An organization is a set of cultural and procedural patterns intended to create valuable results. At any point in time, the organization is driven by its current stakeholders. The reason you are at your job is to get things done.

While this observation may not seem earth-shattering at first, compare it with the generational friction that so often appears in the office.

When a Boomer who works long hours sees a GenXer stroll in to the office at 9:30am, he may assume that the younger worker is lazy. Conversely, the GenXer might assume that the Boomer is just trying to impress the boss, or is extremely inefficient.

Neither one of these accusations is fair. What matters most is the purpose of work: to be productive.

Virtually every conflict between generations is confusion over this issue. When Millennials switch jobs after a year or two, they may be perceived as disloyal. But if work is about getting things done, it makes sense to move somewhere else if you believe you can provide more value.

Likewise, the youngest workers express disappointment when older workers stay at a bad job. This sentiment matches the data: A 2012 study by Netimpact reports a whopping 91% of Millennials consider a positive workplace culture to be a "non-negotiable" when seeking a new job.

But again, their judgment is unfounded. Work is not about having an upbeat culture, it's about *providing value.* If an employee is able to get things done in a workplace with terrible morale, they may not see a reason to leave.

These observations may make sense, but they don't make the process of understanding other generations any easier. The GenXers interest in diversity and inclusion seems to clash directly with the Boomer focus on rewards and status. The Silent Generation's view on hard work and humility seems like an affront to the instant-results, affirmation-seeking mindset of Millennials.

It's not that Millennials are self-centered. They are just used to finding out if they have the right answer, right away.

It's not that GenXers are indecisive. They are just acutely aware of marginalization and thus want to seek consensus.

It's not that Boomers are cutthroat. They are just people who have tasted success and enjoy the recognition of winning.

And it's not that the Silent Generation is unteachable. They are just a group that has the life experience and the patience to take their time to learn what's next.

Each generation sees work differently. Your job is to help them see it from a new perspective—even if only for a moment.

If the fundamental purpose of work is to get things done, the strategy for working with each generation must be to turn the conversation back toward productivity.

That means we need a definition for productivity that works for every perspective and every generation. While we normally consider productivity "getting things done," the truth is that a productive person is not just someone who accomplishes a lot.

Rather, **a productive person is someone whose actions provide real value** to those around them. Sometimes that means being supportive during a crisis. Or, it may mean giving clear answers to difficult questions.

We can't always look at the most visible data points to figure out if someone is being productive. The number of hours worked or the size of the pile of paperwork completed can be deceptive.

What if those hours were wasted? What if those forms were filled out incorrectly?

And just because the word "value" appears in the definition of a productive person, productivity is not always about getting the most money. In a mutually beneficial relationship, value is maximized by ensuring that all parties can communicate clearly and receive what is best for them.

This may seem like a challenge to the viewpoint that some generations hold: companies exist to provide returns for their stockholders. However, *shareholders* are really just one type of *stakeholder*. The best increase in value is one that happens steadily over the long term, rather than unpredictable spikes and valleys.

Everyone provides some kind of value. When we evaluate their contribution, it must be the in context of the larger goals of the organization.

Therefore, the perspective on what others are doing for the organization has to change. We must not assume we can determine their worth purely on their outward appearance.

Generations may see their role at work differently, but each point of view is really a facet of the same idea.

The purpose of work is productivity. We have our jobs to get things done that provide value.

Of course, it's hard to understand how *others* are being productive when *we* are used to working in a particular way.

That's why the telecommuter seems lazy to the person who has always come into the office. That's why the manager who "checks in" on employees seems like they aren't working to someone who prefers to keep their head down and work independently.

That's why the individual who constantly seeks confirmation they are doing things right (and affirmation that they are the right person for the job) can seem overly attention-focused to people used to working without much feedback.

We need to change our perspective on the work others accomplish. We need to become more open-minded to styles of working. We need a new approach for engaging with others, especially those who come from different generations.

We need to change the conversation, but not without a plan for doing so.

We need a new agenda for work.

PART II

ONE PRINCIPLE, THREE TOOLS

The greatest discovery of my generation is that
a human being can alter his life by altering his attitudes.

– William James

Chapter 5

A New Agenda

You are never too old to set another goal
or to dream a new dream.

– C.S. Lewis

IF EVERY GENERATION shares one sentiment in common, it's the notion that they can and will improve the world. Some do so without much fanfare, while others seek immediate recognition. But every generation changes society, develops new technologies, and impacts the culture in a significant way.

The high-minded efforts of each generation's leaders translate to a practical plan. There is work to be done and that generation hopes to do it.

The agenda of every generation is to pursue their own ideas. Every generation insists its dreams are important and relevant.

Because each generational cohort wants to advance their own agenda—and because each agenda is different—there will necessarily be intergenerational conflict.

We can't eliminate this clash. The younger generation will often seem impetuous, lazy, and self-serving to older generations. And those with more experience may seem slow, overcautious and antiquated to some. To quote Adlai Stevenson, "That which seems the height of absurdity in one generation often becomes the height of wisdom in another."

We cannot expect a generation to change its priorities. After all, we cannot demand that an individual abandon their core beliefs, so why would we expect an entire group to do so?

Instead, we should look to build bridges across ages. A new agenda is needed: one based on understanding and respect.

This level of comprehension, however, is not about absorbing everything someone else believes. We are not seeking complete harmony between generations. We are just looking for a way to be more productive at the office.

"Understanding another generation" means understanding their *process* for working. How do they approach work? How do they accomplish tasks? How do they build workplace relationships? And how do they utilize technology?

Likewise, "respecting another generation" does not necessarily mean agreeing with their beliefs and values. For example, as of 2012 the Pew Research center reports that only 44% of Americans aged 65 and up support same-sex marriage, contrasted with 81% of Americans aged 18-29. Generations vehemently disagree on many fundamental issues, and this discord often leads to a lack of respect.

However, the workplace usually doesn't revolve around strident political, moral, and social issues. "Respecting another generation" at the office is about respecting the results they produce. A great sale, a well-crafted report, or compelling resolution to a customer service problem benefits the company regardless of the age of the person responsible. But each generation values results differently. Each cohort uses different frameworks as hallmarks of success.

First up is the Silent Generation. Writing for the Project Management Institute, Conrado Morlan notes that:

> Members of this generation were born pre-World War II. In the United States, this generation grew up in a time of economic turmoil and world conflicts. They set their values on discipline, respect, and self-sacrifice.
>
> For me, it's very important to understand that discipline, loyalty, and working within the system are among the values that members of the Silent Generation will bring to my project team. I have to appreciate that those members have a vast knowledge to share and high standards on work ethic.

Morlan's commentary effectively encapsulates the working style of many individuals born between 1925 and 1945. Their approach to work is to follow the rules and respect existing institutions.

For the Silent Generation, work is not just about what you produce, but also about your humility, your devotion, and your consistency during working hours. If any generation can be aptly compared to a fable, consider this group as the title character in The Tortoise and the Hare.

This is a generation motivated by service.

Moving forward to the Baby Boomers shows an entirely different perspective on work and results. With the economic opportunity afforded by the post-war boom, this cohort tends to equate hard work with limitless potential. The more time you put in at the office, the more rewards you reap.

Boomers, therefore, may be the most competitive generation working today.

In fact, according to a poll conducted by AARP, four in ten members of this generation state they plan to keep working full-time "until they drop."

This is a cohort that is highly social at the office. They stress loyalty in relationships. They expect professional work to consist of structured meetings. Research performed by Knoll, Inc. in 2012 shows that Baby Boomers value "quality of meeting rooms" highest and having an "engaging workplace" the lowest.

For Boomers, success at work is best measured through leadership and authority. Arriving early, staying late, and coming in on the weekend shows commitment and importance. Attending meetings—or better yet, leading them—demonstrates their position in the organization.

In short, many Boomers thrive in a culture of long hours, face-to-face interaction, and reinforced hierarchy.

The generation that followed the Baby Boomers came of age in a world becoming increasingly small through global communication and increasingly more aware of our interconnectedness. The GenXers—many of which were children of Boomers—saw their parents putting in long hours.

A 2004 paper from the Upjohn Institute for Employment Research describes the change in home life for this generation and the next:

> In 1975, the U.S.-licensed child care industry comprised 30,000 child care centers and 81,000 homes…the number of regulated family child care homes increased from nearly 200,000 in 1988 to over 300,000 in 2002; regulated child care centers increased from approximately 86,000 in 1991 to over 116,000 in 2003.

That means dual-income GenXers couples who have children are more likely to seek work-life balance. Many are opting out of families entirely. In fact, the Center For Work-Life Policy reports as of 2011 that 43% of GenX women *do not have children.*

This is a cohort which sees the workplace as a balancing act: it's where some work must be done but it's also what makes their personal life possible.

That's likely why GenXers—having started at work with the first personal computers—are more likely to expect to be able to work from home.

For Generation X, the purpose of work is to fund their personal lives. If GenXers have anything to prove, it's that GenXers *choose* to work.

❖ ❖ ❖ ❖ ❖

The author Alison Maitland sums up the youngest workers as follows:

> The idea of work being an activity and not a place—that is more important to Generation Y.

This claim is supported by the research from Knoll, which shows how Millennials are the opposite of Boomers with regard to priorities. This cohort rated "engaging workplace" the highest and "quality of meeting rooms" the lowest.

Millennials are often characterized as "digital natives." It's likely they used more advanced communication and collaboration technologies *before* entering the workforce than they will see in the first decade of their career.

Most people don't need to see data to know that Millennials prefer texting to talking on the phone. But that doesn't mean this cohort is anti-social. Instead, they experience social dynamics differently. In fact, research performed by the rental company ZipCar in 2010 showed that 45% of this generation "makes a conscious effort to drive less" and 54% "sometimes choose to spend time with friends online instead of driving to see them."

This is also a generation accused of having no work ethic. But writer Cam Marston disagrees:

> Millennial employees are dedicated to completing their tasks well. They have not been raised in a way that demands them to look around and see what should be done next.
>
> Instead they ask "what is my job" and go about figuring the best, fastest way to complete that task. Then they consider themselves done.

For Millennials, work is about the task in front of them. They seek clarity on what results they need to produce and affirmation that the work was completed correctly. According Lauren Stiller Rikleen, this generation measures their respect by being heard, while older workers associate respect with experience and longevity.

Millennials are the work-from-anywhere, play-anytime generation. They aren't disloyal, but they *do* expect the world to change dramatically from one day to the next.

This generation is ready for the next opportunity and is always seeking it out.

Generations have always struggled to communicate. Every age group sees life differently and wants to advance its own agenda.

But the workplace is only a subset of society as a whole. At the office, the factory, or the jobsite, we are not required to solve all the world's problems through heated debate. Instead, we need to get things done to advance the mission of the organization.

That's not to say that companies don't get involved in questions of moral consciousness that are viewed differently by each generation.

But rather, what we need to respect at work is the process of working itself, and the results that each generation values.

The agenda at the workplace must change. It's no longer solely about establishing and advancing the ideas of our generation. After all, we're not alone at the office. We're surrounded by people separated from us by decades.

Instead, the new agenda is one of embracing other generations as providing distinctive and complimentary values at work. That doesn't mean we always agree. But rather, that we find ways to work together.

That's how we build bridges between generations.

That's how we learn to work alongside colleagues from different cohorts.

Now, it's time to learn some tools to make this actually happen.

Chapter 6

The Technology Rubric

We live in a society exquisitely dependent on science and technology, in which hardly anyone knows anything about science and technology.

– Carl Sagan

THERE'S NO WAY TO TALK about improving workplace communications among generations without talking about technology.

This may be the most profound difference in working today versus a few years ago. A 2012 report from the McKinsey Global Institute states that employees spend 25% of their workday battling their email inbox. That's important because most workers remember a time *before email even existed.*

The simplest way to characterize the relationship of each generation to technology is to assume that the younger an individual, the more familiar they are with the latest tools. But in fact, the fastest growing demographic on Facebook since 2010 is women over 55—according to the tech news source Mashable.

The assumption that older people are less capable with technology isn't just wrong—it's dangerous. Believing this reinforces stereotypes and makes it more difficult to work and communicate productively.

Instead, we need an effective tool for understanding how different generations view technology and how to support technology usage

One approach is to use a *rubric.*

The word "rubric" comes from education. It's a tool for measuring student performance that describes expectations for quality, often based on individual background. Rubrics can also be used for reflection and peer-review.

Here's the outline of **The Technology Rubric** for generations at work:

Individuals often think of technology usage in the context of the specific platform or product. For example, people evaluate others as "knowing how to text," "knowing how to use Facebook," or "knowing how to send a fax."

Instead, consider recasting each technology platform into a generational context. For example:

YouTube is a **social media platform** that generates revenue and interconnects people with shared interests through video uploads, comments, social sharing, YouTube channels, and advertisement systems.

However, many generations think of YouTube solely as **motion picture technology.** Reframing the social network as foremost a place to watch video can make this service more palatable.

The Technology Rubric consists of four questions about a particular platform, product, or service:

1. Which historical technology does it most closely resemble?

(Film, Radio, Television, Telegram, Telephone, Fax Machines, Copiers, Cameras, Typewriters, Early Computers)

2. How is the physical and social experience impacted by age and generation?

(Size of visual details and human eyesight, interactions required and human dexterity, complexity of use, and degree to which the experience extends something else familiar)

3. How does the technology mesh with the personality of the generation?

(Does it support private exploration or require public social interaction? How does it handle failure? Is it an inclusive or exclusive technology?)

4. Is the technology immediate, portable, and flexible, or does it require time and particular space to learn and use according to prescribed rules?

(Instant feedback? Time-limited? User-driven?)

Using the Technology Rubric requires answering these questions and looking to generational trends to find out how to interact.

The Rubric itself is as follows:

Questions
1. Which historical technology does it most closely resemble?
(A) Pre 1950: Film, TV, Radio, Telephone, Telegraph, Typewriter, Cameras   (B) 1950-1990: Fax, Digital Cameras, Early Computers, Printers   (C) Does not resemble a historical technology.
Q2. How is the physical/social experience impacted by age/generation?
(D) Physically large and easy-to-read, interface can be used without much dexterity, similar to other technologies.   (E) Smaller and more difficult to read, interface requires some manual dexterity, somewhat similar to other technologies.   (F) Tiny and may be difficult to read for persons without 20-20 vision. Complex interface. Does not resemble older technologies.
3. How does the technology mesh with the generation's personality of the generation?
(G) May be learned/used in private, linear design, few features or options.   (H) Semi-public, facilitates communication/collaboration. Hierarchical.   (I) Highly public and social. Primary use is for sharing and publishing. Rich, layered featureset. Limitless ways to access.
4. Is the technology immediate, portable, and flexible, or does it require time and particular space to learn and use according to prescribed rules?
(J) Not immediately responsive. Usage or availability driven by a schedule and/or a policy. Not portable or usable from anywhere.   (K) Provides some feedback and internal guidance. Always available, but exclusive to certain users. Some flexibility in features.   (L) Instant response and immediate feedback. Allows social mistakes. Can be used anywhere, anytime, by anyone, in many different ways.

Tactics
T1: The closest historical technology can be used as an analogy, or even as a source to borrow terminology for explaining the tool. Each group tends to characterize a new technology as...

Silent Generation	...something familiar from pre-1950. Usage patterns will be highly linear. They may fear they will break the tool if used incorrectly.
Baby Boomers	...something familiar from 1950-1990. Usage patterns will be procedural; Boomers will readily revert to manual methods if needed.
GenXers	...a necessary tool. Will seek training to improve productivity. Expects technology to be routinely updated or replaced.
Millennials	...a matter of course. Searches for workarounds, tips, and hacks. Shares discoveries with friends. Usually distrusts formal technology training.

T2/T3: The physical and social experience of technology varies by each generation according to their personality and values.

Silent Generation	Likely to struggle with small screens and complex, non-linear interfaces. Often patient, willing to learn.
Baby Boomers	Likely to have some challenges with small screens and interfaces. Sometimes distrustful of new tools. Prefers to use technology alone. Often impatient with informal training.
GenXers	Able to adapt quickly to new technologies, but may struggle with complex usage patterns. Happy to learn and use in group settings.
Millennials	Often have instant understanding of interfaces without being able to explain why. Impatient with formal training. Prefers social tools.

T4: Non-portable, slower tools that do not give immediate feedback and have a straightforward use pattern will often be preferred by older generations. Tools that respond instantly, correct mistakes and are highly flexible are preferred by younger generations.

Here's how to use this rubric. When you're installing a new technology at the office, interacting with a colleague who is using a technology, or having a broad discussion about the best way to engage technology across generations, ask each of the four questions.

Then, consider which of the suggested replies applies most readily to the situation.

Finally, review the proposed tactics for each corresponding generational cohort. This should inform your approach to communication as well as your plan for implementation.

For example, consider the following case study:

> The Apogee Courier Service wants to add GPS-enabled routing and tracking to their fleet of local delivery trucks. These devices will provide guidance to drivers on the best routes to use, as well as report back to headquarters if a vehicle gets too far off track.
>
> **Question 1** asks which historical technology the device most closely resembles. Although it might be considered to be similar to a two-way radio to talk to a dispatcher, the GPS units require manual entry of destinations using a keypad. Therefore, this program does not resemble a historical technology. (C)

Question 2 reviews the physical and social experience. Although the GPS device is unfamiliar overall, it does resemble a cellphone in appearance. It has a similar interface in terms of size/complexity. (E)

Question 3 discusses the relationship between the technology and the personality of the generation. The GPS units are somewhat public because they connect with headquarters in real time. However, they do represent a stronger element of control over drivers, so they reinforce the existing company hierarchy. (H)

Question 4 asks about the immediacy, portability, and accessibility of the technology. The boxes will give near-instant feedback, but are only usable in the trucks and have limited functions. (K)

The Tactics section gives advice based on these responses. In this case study, the company has employee drivers from every generation.

Tactic 1 notes that older generations will assume the device can be broken or malfunction. Therefore, a soft rollout might be advisable where the GPS units are first used as a passive electronic map for several months. Younger drivers may see the GPS as an obvious and welcome addition. Or, they may see the program as showing distrust from their employer and seek a workaround that lets them control their own route.

Tactic 2/3 should inform the training program for the GPS units. Given the wide variety in ages and skills with an unfamiliar, physically small, and complex technology, the company may want to use a certification approach where any driver can take a test in lieu of formal education. Expert drivers—particularly those from Generation X—may be asked to lead workshops or teach peers one-on-one.

Tactic 4 explains that the GPS tool's popularity with different generations will likely depend on the quality of the platform selected. The company may want to examine the population of the drivers when making their final purchase.

That's the Technology Rubric! Put it in the back of your mind. Keep thinking about technology and generations. We'll put it to use in Part III. But for now, it's time to talk about talking.

When we're not using technology, how do we have conversations with people of other generations?

Turn the page to find out.

Chapter 7

The Conversation Map

The young do not know enough to be prudent,
and so they attempt the impossible,
and achieve it, generation after generation.

– Pearl S. Buck

PERHAPS THE MOST IMMEDIATE CHALLENGE when interacting with other generations is knowing what to say.

After all, speaking to others usually requires thinking on our feet rather than following a recipe.

Most individuals in the workplace, however, have had some experience with books and media that require genuine interactivity.

Baby Boomers may remember *TutorText*. Children of Generation X may recall a series called *Choose Your Own Adventure*. And of course some Millennials had the chance to play adventure-based video games.

All of these historical inventions are forms of interactive literature, where the reader (or user) decides what to do and discovers what happens next.

If you've never used one of these formats, here's an excerpt from *The Cave of Time* by Edward Packard:

> You walk into the interior of the strange cavern; then wait while your eyes become accustomed to the dim, amber light. Gradually you can make out the two tunnels. One curves downward to the right; the other leads upward to the left.
>
> If you take the tunnel leading to the left, turn to page 20.
>
> If you take the tunnel leading to the right, turn to page 61.

Part of the reason that interactive fiction is so engaging is because the reader has some sense of control. The same principle applies for the next tool in your intergenerational communication toolbox. It's called **The Conversation Map** for generations.

Here's how it works: Pick one of these four starting scenarios, and then follow the prompts to decide where to go next.

You're standing at the water cooler, talking about the company reorganization with some of your colleagues. If most of them are: • Silent Generation, turn to B.   • Baby Boomers, turn to C.   • GenXers, turn to D.   • Millennials, turn to C.
You're in a staff meeting and want to present an idea that you think will improve productivity. If the person leading the meeting is: • Silent Generation, turn to B.   • Baby Boomers, turn to E.   • GenXers, turn to F.   • Millennials, turn to G.
You've received an email from another division which asks a question about policy that you are not sure how to answer. If the group you need to ask is mostly: • Silent Generation, turn to H.   • Baby Boomers, turn to I.   • GenXers, turn to F.   • Millennials, turn to G.
You're sitting down with your supervisor to discuss a complaint from a customer. If your supervisor is from the: • Silent Generation, turn to B.   • Baby Boomers, turn to K.   • GenXers, turn to L.   • Millennials, turn to J.

A. Remember, this generation is accustomed to hierarchy and institutions. Avoid ending a conversation without asking permission.
B. This is a generational cohort that may fear becoming obsolete due to new changes and updates. Before discussing the components of any new proposal, consider restating how you value their experience.
C. This generational will often see major organizational changes as a chance to move ahead. If you are: • Silent Generation, turn to B. • Baby Boomer, turn to H. • GenXer, turn to D. • Millennial, turn to G.
D. This generation may see changes or mandates as frustrating or unnecessary. An admission that the change is probably out of your control and a desire to get back to work will likely be a relief.
E. Presenting a suggestion in front of others without warning may be construed as disrespectful. Ask for a private meeting first to discuss. And, also turn to A.
F. Be prepared to analyze the idea in detail. But be aware, if most of the other members are: • S lent Generation, turn to B. • Baby Boomers, turn to A. • GenXers, turn to D. • Millennials, turn to G.
G. Th s generation is clarity-driven and action-oriented and would often rather try something as an experiment than have a long conversation. This should inform how you bring up the issue in the first place.
H. Keep in mind that this is a generation tends to prefer in-person conversations which give them a chance to discuss their experience and how it is relevant to the issue at hand.
I. This generation considers itself decisive and competent. Even though you may think you know the answer before asking, they will feel appreciated if you make the effort to ask them in person for advice.
J. This generation is not likely to want to dwell on the problem or the relationship. In fact, turn to G.
K. Apologize and focus on the importance of repairing the long-term customer relationship. However, also keep in mind that...turn to E.
L. Their reaction may be one where they feel that problem cannot be solved. If so, turn to D. However, if they think a solution might be poss ble—especially using new technologies or more modern procedures—this generation will likely want to call a meeting to discuss. Turn to F.

The Conversation Map doesn't cover all situations. And like any aspect of generational theory, it doesn't prescribe what will happen every time.

However, it can be a useful tool for thinking about how best to react to other people based on their cohort— as well as your own. You can also use it to prepare for an important meeting, increasing the value of that meeting and your potential success in that interaction.

You can create your own conversation maps as well. To do this, consider each generation in terms of the types of conversations they want to have:

✓ Millennials seek conversations that are brief, focused on immediate activity, and affirm that they are doing the right thing.

✓ GenXers want to have conversations that are inclusive of all perspectives and opinions. They are willing to wait longer to make sure everyone has a chance to say their piece.

✓ Boomers tend toward conversations that help express their status and role in the organization. They want to show their experience and their capability at the same time.

✓ Members of the Silent Generation often use conversations to tell stories. Many times this is done in order demonstrate their emphasis on devotion, self-sacrifice, and relevance.

It's not easy to talk to someone from another generational cohort.

In fact, it's not always easy to talk to someone your own age.

But what matters is not what is said first, but where you take the conversation.

What matters is the map you use, the route you take, and the destination you ultimately reach.

Use the conversation map. Anticipate what might be coming.

Plan what you're going to say, so you can say the right thing at the right time.

Chapter 8

The Workflow Distributor

True success comes only when every generation
continues to develop the next generation.

– John Maxwell

THE FIRST TOOL was about understanding how different generations view technology. The second focused on effective methods for having productive conversations across different age groups.

But once you've decided what hardware and software to use—and figured out what to say—how do you actually get work done?

The term *workflow* is often used to describe the sequence of processes through which a piece of work moves from initial idea to final completion.

For example, in a factory workflow starts out with a customer order, arrival of raw materials, manufacturing, testing, packaging, and finally delivery. Each piece of the workflow is done by different people in different teams.

But even though these groups are separate, they are all connected. They all must work together in order to ensure that the product is finished correctly and on time.

Unfortunately, many critical operations in many companies don't go nearly as smoothly as a highly efficient factory. Consider the following two fundamental questions:

> If there is work to be done, who should be the one do it?

> If work is assigned to someone else, what role do you have in that work?

Not surprisingly, every person and every generation tends to have a different view on these two questions. What are people likely to say?

- ✓ **Silent Generation:** "If there is work to be done, the person who is assigned to do it should complete that work. My job is to make sure I'm not in their way, but to be helpful if asked."

- ✓ **Baby Boomers:** "For any work that has to be done, if you want it done right, you often just have to do it yourself. And if someone else is doing the work, I probably need to keep an eye on it—or pitch in/take it over if there are any problems."

- ✓ **GenXers:** "If work has to be done, everyone who is impacted should have a role in helping to get 'across the finish line.' And even if a piece of work is not my job, being helpful and supportive of others is always part of my job."

- ✓ **Millennials:** "If there is work to be done, why can't there be a system to do it for us? If it's not my job, doesn't getting involved distract me from what I'm supposed to be doing?"

The Workflow Distributor is a tool for deciding how to assign tasks to other people using generational perspectives as a guide. Here's how it works:

For any given task, consider four dimensions:

Is the task **difficult,** especially due to complexity and urgency?

Does the task make use of specialized **skills?**

Is the task something that requires long stretches of **uninterrupted time?**

Is there **clarity** in the process of executing the task and the desired outcome?

Then, select the two elements which seem most significant—where you score the task the lowest or the most highest.

For example, if a task is particularly difficult (D), you might consider it to be a "High D." If a task does not require a great deal of focused time, it might be a "Low T."

After answering all four questions as "high" or "low," decide which of the two elements best characterizes defines the task at hand.

Then, look up the two scores on The Workflow Distributor on the following page:

		Skill Required		Time		Clarity	
		Low	High	Low	High	Low	High
Difficulty	Low	a	a,b	c	a,d	e	g
	Hi	f	f,h	f	e,a	f	a,g
Skill	Low			c	a,e	d	a
	Hi			a,g	b	d	g
Time	Low					f	c
	Hi					e	a

Each grid intersection lists one or two reflections, in order of preference, which matches to the following list:

a. Often best performed members of the Silent Generation, as they often characterize good work through devotion and self-sacrifice. Members of this cohort often appreciate the chance to show their value where others will not.
b. Often well-suited to GenXers, who appreciate the chance to use their specialization in a low stress task.
c. Best for Millennials, who can multi-task easily on quick, straightforward assignments.
d. Matches well with Boomers, who value working long hours on projects they know they can complete.
e. Good for GenXers, who do not mind exploring tasks if they are not under a great deal of pressure.
f. Often best for Boomers, as a challenging, poorly-defined task can show their leadership skills.
g. Best for Millennials, who appreciate direct instructions and clear feedback that they are on the right path.
h. Matches with GenXers interest in doing difficult work under pressure if they are uniquely qualified to do so.

Here's how to use The Workflow Distributor. Consider a case in which the company has decided to improve customer service by having someone answer the phone directly, rather than using an automated system. Reviewing each of the questions:

> Is the task **difficult,** especially due to complexity and urgency?

Certainly this is not the case at all. This work is extremely straightforward. (Low)

> Does the task make use of specialized **skills?**

Answering the phone will require considerable knowledge of company products and policies, plus how to use the phone system to route calls appropriately. (High)

> Is the task something that requires long stretches of **uninterrupted time?**

Typically, calls will only last for a minute or two until they are transferred to another person. And since the company has not had someone to answer the phone in the past, it's not likely that many calls will come in during the course of an hour. (Low)

> Is there **clarity** in the process of executing the task and the desired outcome?

Yes. In fact, the company might write out scripts and conduct some sample calls to determine best practices for customer service. (High)

Of all of these responses, the Low Difficulty/High Skill comparison can be construed as the most meaningful pair. This implies that a member of the Silent Generation, or possibly a GenXer, might be the right employee for this task.

Like all aspects of generational theory, The Workflow Distributor is not perfect. However, it can be a starting point for determining how someone might react to a particular task or better interpreting their performance in their current role.

The purpose of the tool is to promote understanding. It may guide a manager in assigning work or a colleague in better supporting those around them.

Gaining an understanding of how other cohorts view work is essential to improving intergenerational relations.

Developing a respect for what others value as results helps build a bridge between ages.

Now you know the tools. You have a Technology Rubric, a Conversation Map, and a Workflow Distributor.

It's time to see the tools in action.

That's the purpose of Part III.

PART III

STORIES AND SOLUTIONS

This future is ours to embrace.
Whether we, the established generations,
choose to accept that is in our court.

– Rosario Dawson

Chapter 9

The New Executive

One generation plants the trees,
and another gets the shade.

– Chinese Proverb

WHEN THE DIVISION VICE PRESIDENT finally retired, all two hundred employees in the building started whispering. No one else had held the top spot in over fifteen years. In fact, more than two-thirds of the current employees had never known anyone else to be in that corner office.

Many of the managers expected that someone among them would be moved up by headquarters. Or perhaps another vice president would be relocated. They were almost all Baby Boomers, and most were highly competitive. Someone was about to be the top dog, which they assumed meant *everything* would change.

That's why it was such a surprise when the announcement came down that Sheila Taylor—former CFO of the company's most recent acquisition—would be the new division vice president. No one had met her and not many people claimed they were happy with the choice. Many expected that one of them would be promoted.

On Sheila's first day, the various managers changed their daily routes throughout the building to get a look at her. She was in her early 30s, and was quietly unpacking her belongings. A few tried to go in and make small talk, but Sheila patiently explained to each one that she wanted to schedule a meeting with each manager individually rather than have informal conversations on her first day.

That didn't make the managers happy. But word spread among the younger employees, especially the GenXers and the Millennials. They were excited that someone so young would be running the office. Later that day, Sheila sent out an email to the entire division.

To: South Division – All

From: Sheila Taylor

Subject: Hello from Sheila

Hi everyone! I'm excited to take on this new role as your Division Vice President. You're probably wondering why the company chose me for this position. The main reason I am here is because of the recent acquisition of my former employer, Garland Products. My primary objective is to help the company pilot some of the best practices and systems from Garland here in the South Division.

Of course, the first thing I need to do is to get to know all of you. I'll be meeting with everyone in the building—that's right, all of you!—one on one in the next few weeks.

I look forward to chatting with each of you.

Thanks!

Sheila

Everyone in the company reacted differently to this email. The older members of the company wondered why the new VP didn't do what the old one did every quarter: give a speech. And along with many of the managers, they were skeptical about her plan to talk to every person in the building. What a waste of time!

The younger generations saw things differently. A few were excited about the chance to talk directly with the VP. Some had been there for years and were confident Sheila's predecessor didn't even know their names. A few of the Millennials hoped to present their ideas for improving company culture and wanted to ask about the possibility of telecommuting.

And some people of all ages started thinking about the new leader as a chance to report on people who they felt were not contributing very much.

The new executive likely had no idea what was coming.

Sheila began her one-on-one meetings the next day. Each would last thirty minutes, and she started with the first person she came across: Bill, a 38 year-old IT specialist.

Although Bill was happy to have the chance to talk to the boss, he couldn't help but feel annoyed. He was in the middle of a major upgrade project to the backup systems when Sheila arrived. His office was covered in disassembled computer parts.

"I'm Sheila, the new division VP," she explained. "I hope you got my email. I am hoping to have a chance to talk to everyone in the building, and I'd like to start with you if that's okay."

Bill didn't know what to say. He wished she had scheduled an appointment, but she was the new boss. "Sure."

For the next few minutes, Sheila asked a series of increasingly specific questions. She began with general questions about what Bill thought the division did best, as well as where it needed improvement. But pretty soon she was asking about his job, including the obstacles he faced personally.

Although Bill wanted to reply honestly, he didn't feel safe in doing so. Instead, he talked about generic issues with budget and resources. Sheila walked down the hall a few minutes later. But before Bill could get back to work on the backup system, there was another person in his doorway. It was Diana from the billing department.

An older lady with nearly thirty years of experience at the company, Diana was there to complain *again* about Anil, one of the members of Bill's technical support team.

"I've called him twice and left voicemails both times. He never picks up the phone!"

Bill sighed and thought for a moment about the kid, who had just turned twenty years old. *Have you tried using the online help system? Or better yet, just rebooting your computer?*

But he said, "I'll talk to him, Diana. Sorry for the inconvenience."

She left, rolling her eyes. Then Bill went to his computer to write an email to Anil.

Later that day, Sheila happened to arrive at Diana's cubicle. Of course, she had no idea about Diana's talk with Bill in IT.

"I'm Sheila," she introduced herself.

"Of course you are!" Diana replied. "It's so lovely to meet you. Please, sit down!"

"You know, when I started at this company in 1984 it was my first professional job. The boys were grown by that point, and so I went back to school and got an accounting certificate. But I never imagined, well, I never would have imagined back then that a woman would be in the big corner office! And so young!"

Sheila smiled. "Thank you. I appreciate that."

Before Diana could continue, Sheila pointed to an old photograph on the desk. "Is that you?"

"Why yes, that's me and Ralph on our wedding day. Ralph thought it would be fun to drive an old Studebaker from when we were kids away from the church. You know that car company didn't last long after that. Our marriage has done a bit better."

Sheila laughed. "I know what you mean. My grandfather had an old car like that. I remember that he would never drive it too hard. Had to let the engine cool down completely before restarting it. I think he was superstitious."

"Really? How funny."

"I guess technology hasn't changed. If my computer is being funny, that's the first thing I do. Shut it down completely. Give it a few minutes to cool off. Or maybe that's giving *me* a few minutes to cool off. Then I restart it."

"Huh." said Diana. "Maybe I should do the same. Now, dear, what did you want to talk about?"

Sheila's last meeting of the day was with Richard. Although he only joined the company five years before, he led the sales team. Richard was a few years past fifty and had over twenty five years of experience, which he would tell anyone whether they asked or not.

He had a neat, handwritten stack of index cards ready for the conversation. And although Richard had figured his last three record-setting years would have earned him this job, he tried not to show his feelings during the meeting. Instead, he focused on the opportunities he saw for the division and suggestions for Sheila's leadership.

"Our main problem here," Richard explained, "is a lack of discipline. Of course I need my reps selling, and that means they need to be out of the office. But they should be coming in every morning and returning at the end of the day to give an update."

"And the problem is worse in other departments. Sure, the employees are here all the time, but they aren't always working. Or at least not working hard enough. Marketing seems to be always behind on updating our spec sheets. And the engineering guys never give us quotes when we need them. Maybe you need to hire more engineers, but I don't think that's the real problem, if you know what I mean."

Richard had been talking nearly constantly for fifteen minutes when Sheila finally spoke up. "Richard, it sounds like you are a very observant person. You've got a perspective which I haven't heard yet today. And I appreciate that."

"You're welcome, Sheila. Somebody ought to tell it like it is, I figure."

"Thank you." Sheila replied. "I was wondering if I might have your permission to pause our conversation right now and return to it later. I feel like I might be better equipped to understand some of your views after I've had a chance to speak to more people."

He nodded.

"And in addition, I think some of your notes might make an excellent report to orient me to the challenges ahead. Is that something you'd like to write up?"

"Absolutely."

"Thank you again. I appreciate your candor and your expertise. I'll take the next two weeks to meet with others, and then come back to you. Please get me that report as soon as you can. Thank you for your time."

"No problem, Sheila. No problem at all."

With that, they shook hands and Richard returned to his notes. *If I get started now, I may be able to finish before midnight.*

The story of *The New Executive* features several elements of generational traits and intergenerational conflicts. The characters also make use of strategies built on the tools in Part II for making conversations more productive.

Early in the narrative, Sheila (GenXer) demonstrates her generation's **focus on inclusion.** Instead of starting by reviewing the books or talking with her top managers, she decides to meet with every person in the division one-on-one. In fact, she even avoids making small talk with people who come to visit her, demonstrating that she wants to be fair and not play favorites.

The middle managers (Baby Boomers) tend to associate value at work with **status and authority.** That's why they want to talk to her up front, and why they think her plan to meet with all of the employees is a waste of time.

The front line employees (Millennials) are excited that a new boss means the possibility of change. They are particularly interested in **company culture** as well as **separating work from place** through telecommuting.

Sheila's first conversation with Bill (GenXer), the IT specialist, shows a generational conflict between people of roughly the same age. Both characters have a desire to be **tolerant and consensus-seeking**, which means they end up speaking at a time which is inconvenient for Bill. That's also why Sheila's questions are about Bill's perspective on the division, rather than about his competence in his role.

Because Bill doesn't want to upset Sheila, he doesn't answer honestly about his concerns. And before he can get back to work, Diana (Silent Generation) shows up. She is frustrated about Anil (Millennial), who seems **averse to speaking on the phone**. This conflict arises because Diana prefers to **use familiar technologies** which enable her to show value through storytelling.

Again, Bill avoids conflict to **show tolerance** by failing to mention the online help system, or the usual suggestion to reboot the computer. Then he goes back to the computer to relay the conversation to Anil using that **employee's preferred technology.**

Later, Sheila (GenXer) and Diana (Silent Generation) are speaking. Diana begins to **tell her story** to express her value. Sheila embraces and redirects (using The Conversation Map) by referencing the photograph on her desk. Then, she relates the care of an old car to an old computer, suggesting that frequent reboots may improve performance (The Technology Rubric). Perhaps Sheila and Anil had a conversation earlier that morning.

Finally, Sheila meets with Richard (Baby Boomer). As someone from a particularly **competitive** generation, he is jealous of her new job. Richard also explains company problems in terms of weaknesses of character, rather than skills.

Sheila needs to reframe their discussion, so she praises Richard's **authority and competence**. Then she asks for permission (using The Conversation Map) to end the meeting and return to it later. Next, Sheila identifies a task that would be well suited to Richard's perspective and generation (using The Workflow Distributor) and again shows her **emphasis on inclusion** when asking him if he *wants* to write that report. Richard then starts immediately with an expectation of staying late into the night, showing his generation's take on **working long hours**.

There may be a new executive coming to your company. Or, you may be the boss that was recently hired.

Alternately, you might identify with one of the characters Sheila encountered in her interviews.

But no matter where you connect, it's likely that part of this story rings true. There are choices everyone has to make, no matter their generation.

Just like the decision that appears in Chapter 10.

Chapter 10

Vetting the Agency

A man is not old until regrets take the place of dreams.

– John Barrymore

MARCUS LOOKED AROUND THE ROOM. It was a big meeting. There was José, the director of product development and recent grandfather. Alexis and Dana, who were both in their early 20s, sat next to their boss with their iPads. Jacqueline, the Chief Information Officer, wore a bright blue suit that offset her gray hair. She also had a couple of the guys from IT with her. And of course Frank, the company, founder, President and CEO was there. His granddaughter Mercedes was there taking notes. She made Alexis and Dana look old. Lastly, he spotted a couple of the guys from the legal department as well.

Marcus was only 35, but he felt lucky to be invited. He was the only person from compliance, since the director was out on vacation. Frank stood up to address those assembled.

"This is a major step for CalCorp," he began. "I started this company when I was 22. I expected my son Roger would take it over when I retired, but instead he's running our London office."

He gestured to the speaker phone. A voice from within replied, "Like Dad would ever retire."

Scattered chuckles echoed in the room. Frank groaned. "Anyway…so now we're launching a brand new marketing initiative. It's bigger—way bigger than anything we've ever done. I should know. I've seen the budget."

More laughter filled the crowded space. Frank Callahan continued speaking. "I can't begin to understand what these companies are proposing. It sounds like a TV commercial but they are calling it a—what is it Mercedes?"

"A multi-modal campaign", she replied, not even looking up from her phone. Her grandfather sighed as he looked back, since he assumed she was not paying attention.

She swiped her thumb across the tiny screen expertly. Then she read: "A multi-modal campaign driven through time-delayed triggering events, user-generated content, and culminating in a viral, Superbowl teaser spot leading to an online, self-hosted conversion portal."

After a solid ten seconds of silence, one of the attorneys spoke up. "All I got from that was *superbowl*."

Laughter burst out and people began talking to one another. Marcus turned to Jacqueline, the CIO.

"I think I understood a little of that, but why am I here? Why are you here? What does marketing have to with compliance or IT?"

She nodded, and turned to one of the members of her team.

Meanwhile, Mercedes tried to show her phone to her grandfather. "See, I have the entire proposal right here. I read the PDF on the train this morning."

Frank attempted to touch the screen to guide the presentation forward but accidentally scraped his finger across the home button.

"I broke it," he apologized.

"No, it's fine," Mercedes replied, exasperated. "Look, I'm sure somebody has a hard copy. Or I can print one for you now."

While Mercedes began working her phone, Dana, the 22-year old from Product Development was talking to José, her boss.

"Is that the original they sent over?"

"Yeah," he replied. "It's really nice."

The shipping package included several physical copies of the proposal, which were professionally bound and printed on high-gloss paper.

Alexis picked up the mailer. "Hey, there's a DVD in here. Looks like it got stuck to the inside of the box."

Within a minute, she had Frank's attention. "Mr. Callahan, I know you've been through a lot of proposals before but this one includes a DVD. Do you think we should watch it?"

Frank nodded, and in a few minutes the room was dark and an image appeared on the big screen.

Marcus spoke up, "Hey Roger, can you see this?"

"See what?" the disembodied voice replied.

"Good point," Jacqueline interjected. A few button pushes later, and Roger indicated he could see the video as well from the office in the UK.

"Incredible!" exclaimed Frank when he realized what was happening. "Okay, roll film!"

The Beckman/Miller logo flashed and then faded away. Firm principal and advertising legend Al Miller appeared, and began speaking against an ocean backdrop.

"I'm taking a break from retirement to thank the team at CalCorp for considering Beckman/Miller for this campaign. And since I'm the oldest person still on the payroll, I have the honor of telling you a little bit about what we're proposing."

The image changed to a series of videos in a grid pattern. Miller's voice over continued.

"Of course you're familiar with some of our work. We've done hundreds of international television advertising campaigns, including a spot in every Superbowl for the last fifteen years. And we won Campaign of the Decade from Advertiser Magazine for our bicycle messenger program in 2003. Which, incidentally, is credited with increasing Solomon Cycles market share by 350%."

"So what are we proposing for CalCorp? At the heart of this campaign is a traditional television commercial to be run during halftime at the biggest sporting event of the year."

"But the world of advertising has changed. Now, we can't just describe a product. We have to *tell a story*. And we also know that people don't just watch the commercial once and then talk about it at the office on Monday."

"In fact, if you're watching this video in a room with some of your team, you'll probably notice that many people are also on their cellphones at the same time. They may be on a laptop or a tablet. That's something we can leverage in telling *your* story."

"Forty years ago, we ran some of the first multi-channel marketing campaigns. It was pretty primitive in those days. We'd run a spot on TV and have spokesperson say 'see our advertisement in Ladies Home Journal.'"

"But now, our multi-channel—or multi-modal—campaigns are much more sophisticated. We're in tons of different places, with text, audio, video, and interactivity. We're on social media as well as traditional media."

"This DVD contains some case studies on other campaigns we've run in the past. And the document outlines some of our ideas for CalCorp."

"We'd love to work with you. Take a look and let us know if you have any questions. As for me, I'm heading back to the beach."

Then, the screen went blank.

"Cool," squawked Roger over the speakerphone.

Frank replied. "Yes. So, José, it was your idea to bring us all here for this meeting. What's next?"

José turned to the young women sitting next to him who worked for him in Product Development. "Actually, it was Dana and Alexis that came up with this. They even suggested your names to be here."

"Really?" Frank raised his eyebrows. He had always tried to respect everyone in his company, but this seemed a little odd. "Dana? Alexis?"

The two of them started to talk at the same time, until Dana finally spoke up. "This proposal affects all of us. I mean, if we're going to going to hire Beckman/Miller, it's like, a huge deal."

Alexis took over. "Obviously they have to know our product line inside and out, which is why we're here. And the whole proposal is based around 'self-hosted' content. That means they think we should put all this stuff— videos, webpages, audio, email, everything—up on *our* servers. So that's why Jacqueline—I mean, uh—Ms. Campbell—and her guys are here. I mean can we do that?"

Marcus chimed in. "Of course. And considering how much regulation we have to follow just for labeling and usage instructions, well, that's why I'm here."

"Right!" Alexis nearly squealed. "And Carson and Kent from the legal department, same reason."

There was a prolonged moment where everyone just looked at the two twenty-somethings sitting next to José. Finally, Frank Callahan broke the silence.

"Okay. If I'm going to appro—" he corrected himself. "If *we're* going to do this, we've got a lot of ground to cover."

He picked up the stack of printed documents, and passed them to his granddaughter to be distributed.

"Let's get started."

In *Vetting the Agency*, a meeting is held among a large group of professionals from a wide variety of backgrounds and generations. The interactions highlight significant distinctions between the characters but ultimately lead to productive resolutions.

The story opens with Marcus (GenXer) surveying the room. He feels lucky to be there, and was only invited because his director—probably a few years older and perhaps more **protective of information**—is out on vacation.

Most of the meeting is led by Frank (Silent Generation), the company founder, president and CEO. His first words are pure **storytelling**, even though he is providing information that everyone in the meeting probably already knows.

After some teasing through the speakerphone from Roger (GenXer), Frank asks a question to his granddaughter Mercedes (Millennial). He becomes irritated that she appears to be ignoring him, but she is actually using her mobile phone as a resource in the meeting (The Technology Rubric). After reading the full passage, she ends up trying to show Frank how to use the phone but he is unsuccessful due to the **fine motor control** required to operate the device.

In the meantime, Dana and Alexis (Millennials) started looking through the original packet as their generation tends to be **action-oriented**. They discover a DVD, validate Frank's experience (The Conversation Map) and get it displayed on the projection screen themselves (The Workflow Distributor).

Before the video is started, Marcus (GenXer) asks if Roger can see the screen as well, due to his generation's emphasis on making sure **everyone is included**.

Frank calls out "roll film!" (The Technology Rubric) and Al Miller (Silent Generation) appears on the screen. Consistent with his generation's spirit of **devotion and self-sacrifice**, he has come out of retirement to "have the honor" of introducing the proposal.

Al outlines the credibility of his firm, emphasizing their **experience and competence**. Then he explains the overall proposal by analogies to historical approaches that older audiences will be able to recognize. (The Technology Rubric). When Al wraps up his introduction, he reminds the audience that he is actually retired.

Frank then asks José (Baby Boomer) about the agenda for the meeting. Recognizing that his colleagues Dana and Alexis (Millennials) are motivated by **affirmation**, he admits it was their idea and gives them the floor. They mutually explain their logic for everyone's presence.

Marcus, wanting to participate in the affirmation, jumps in to show that he understands and appreciates their point of view. The story ends with Frank changing his choice of words. Instead of describing how he will make the decision alone, he acknowledges the multiple generations and stakeholders in the room (The Conversation Map) to show that the decision will be mutual.

❖ ❖ ❖ ❖ ❖

It's not likely that your company will be considering a "multi-modal marketing campaign" centered around a Superbowl commercial. But you *will* participate in meetings with multiple generations.

Managing those interactions means being prepared to think about how other cohorts may view you and your role.

You'll benefit from studying The Technology Rubric, The Conversation Map, and The Workflow Distributor.

But most of all, you'll run better meetings if you're open to other points of view.

Differences matter. And there may be no place where generational differences are more apparent than on the retail sales floor.

That's the topic of Chapter 11.

Chapter 11

A Retail Sales Experience

The ultimate test of man's conscience may be his willingness to sacrifice something today for future generations whose words of thanks will not be heard.

– Gaylord Nelson

Marissa and Deborah started at *Her Way*, the casual clothing store, at about the same time. Marissa had just finished her freshman year in college and was there for a summer job. But Deborah was in her late sixties. Her husband had been out of work for over a year, so she took the job to help supplement her retirement income from her first career as a teacher.

Both women had the same title and the same job function. They both earned the same salary and had overlapping shifts. But in every other regard, they couldn't be more different.

This became apparent when the secret shoppers came through their store.

Neither Marissa nor Deborah had any idea this was happening. They had been told during their orientation that *Her Way* occasionally used third-party professionals to review their customer service. They always used the same script, asked for the same items, and made the same purchases.

The first woman arrived on a Monday afternoon, having freshly memorized the role. Deborah was working in the section where Janine pretended to be browsing.

"That's a great color!" Deborah said as she approached. "Are you looking for anything in particular?"

"Actually," she commented. "I wanted to buy the Thomas Alano khakis. I have a 25% off coupon but I think I left it at home. Can you get me a size 10?"

Deborah paused. She didn't like responding in this way, but she knew it was what she was supposed to do: "I can help you find that size, but we do need you to present the coupon to get the price. It's our policy."

The woman looked frustrated. "Really? It's your coupon that you guys sent me. I just forgot it. And I think it expires today anyway, it's not like I can use it tomorrow."

Again, Deborah stopped for a minute. This customer was perhaps in her mid-thirties, but she reminded Deborah of her elementary students. "A rule is a rule. Do you want my help finding that size 10?"

"Yeah," she replied with a huff.

Deborah went to another display while the woman followed in silence. She flicked through the rack and found the right size. Meanwhile, Marissa was having an entirely different conversation with another pseudo-customer a few dozen feet away.

As the woman looked at some merchandise, Marissa refolded some shirts. "Holler if you need anything, Miss" she called across the store.

"Actually," the woman said, walking toward Marissa. "I wanted to buy the Thomas Alano khakis. I have a 25% off coupon but I think I left it at home. Can you get me a size 10?"

"Sure thing," Marissa replied. "You need 'em now or are you still looking at sweaters?"

"Um," the secret shopper hesitated. "I think just the pants."

"Cool," said Marissa. She pointed at the rack with her eyes, and at the large sign reading ALANO. "They are right over there. Just let me finish this shirt and I'll be right behind you."

The woman, not sure of how to react, began walking away. Marissa finished up her task and nearly sprinted to catch up.

"These are *never* in order," Marissa explained as she began to examine the pants. Then, she slid a large stack toward the customer. "Here, you want to take a look?"

Within a few seconds, the two women had exhausted the supply. "Sorry," said Marissa. "But we did just get a new order in, which will totally have a size 10. You want to meet me at the register, or did you want to try them on in the fitting room?"

"The register."

"Okie dokie."

While Marissa was in the back, Deborah helped her customer to check out.

"Let's see here," Deborah said. She fumbled with the price scanner and the micro-terminal. "Hang on, I'm still learning the system."

It took her a few seconds to read the labels on the buttons and navigate through the system.

"How will you be paying?"

"Credit card," the woman replied. "But before I do, is it possible to ask a manager about that 25% off? It was the whole reason I came in."

Deborah was frozen. "Uh…yeah. Hang on."

She was in the middle of the transaction but was not entirely sure how to cancel the sale. Deborah picked up a handful of loose tags and laid them onto the keypad.

"Be right back." Deborah went looking for her supervisor. The customer wandered toward a sale rack to pass the time.

A moment later, Marissa arrived at the register. She called out to her customer and held up the pants. Then she noticed a second pair, same size, resting on the counter.

When the woman arrived, Marissa said: "Want to get a second pair? You know we have our anytime, buy one, get the second one half off deal."

"Sure."

"Cool." Marissa noticed the pile of tags on the keypad.

"Weird," she muttered, brushing them off. She reset the terminal without thinking about it and typed up the transaction in a flash. "How you paying?"

"Credit card," the woman replied. "But before I do, is it possible to get that 25% off? It was the whole reason I came in."

"Oh," said Marissa. "Well, you're supposed to have the coupon. But I think it's the last day. Let me see."

She looked in the drawer to find another 25% off coupon from a previous customer. "Now, this will only apply to the first one, but still, you're getting a deal!"

"Thanks."

Marissa ran the transaction, bagged the two pairs of pants, and went back to folding shirts.

When Deborah returned with information from the manager, she went to her customer and explained that she would be able to honor the coupon this one time. But when the two of them returned to the checkout counter, the pants that they had left there were gone.

The secret shopper shrugged and left.

A Retail Sales Experience is a story about two secret shoppers and two unwitting employees. The retail workers are both women, both equally experienced in their jobs and both serving in the same role.

But they come from different generations and interact differently.

Deborah (Silent Generation) meets the first customer who immediately asks for an exception to store policy. Because Deborah's perspective is one that tends to **respect rules and institutions**, she feels obligated to push back against this request. When the conversation becomes more confrontational, Deborah feels she is **not being respected as an elder**, but nevertheless is **dutiful** in completing her assigned task. (The Workflow Distributor)

In the meantime, Marissa (Millenial) also encounters a secret shopper pretending to be a customer. But instead of approaching her as instructed in training, her **communication is highly informal**. When the woman talking to Marissa indicates she does have a need, Marissa continues to multitask. Consistent with her generation, she **expects others to be self-sufficient.** Once she wraps up what she is working on, Marissa sprints to catch up, thus **maximizing her use of time**. Similarly, Marissa enlists the customer in finding the right size to be more efficient.

Once at the checkout counter, Deborah has some trouble using the electronic register (The Technology Rubric). When the customer interrupts her to ask again about an exception for the discount, she decides to **appeal to authority** rather than making a decision on her own. Unsure how to cancel the transaction, Deborah leaves the machine and the counter as-is while she seeks help.

Marissa arrives at the same counter, and again calls to her customer across the store. She then makes a **snap decision** when she sees another identical pair of khakis to upsell the customer, followed by rifling through the drawers to find an extra coupon. She rapidly keys in the transaction (The Technology Rubric) and goes back to folding shirts.

When Deborah finally returns, the pants she left on the counter are gone.

This final story shows two completely different customer service experiences.

It's not easy to say which one is better. Although Marissa's customer did buy more, she also did not receive much direct attention. And while Deborah's customer left the store without making a purchase, their interactions were much more cordial. Deborah also adhered to her training and followed store policy.

The point of *A Retail Service Experience* is to show that each generation is different. Even in a relatively consistent interaction with a secret shopper, two individuals presented totally divergent styles of interaction.

When you work with other generations, you're likely to see the same thing. Furthermore, your own generation is likely to affect how you behave.

It doesn't just happen at a casual clothing boutique.

Intergenerational issues can arise in any workplace, at any time.

Are you ready to tackle them?

Afterword: Renewed Relationships

Every generation sees itself differently.

Every generation sees other generations differently.

The goal of intergenerational conversation is not total harmony. It's not complete understanding and unfailing respect.

That's not possible, nor is it reasonable.

But at the workplace, we can put aside the differences in each of our cohorts.

We can focus on what really matters: how we work, and what we value.

Boomers can learn to accept that Millennials view work as an activity, not a place.

GenXers can learn to respect that Boomers value competition and can lead effectively through earned authority.

Members of the Silent Generation don't need to fear becoming obsolete. And members of every generation don't need to focus solely on advancing what they think is right.

With a new agenda, new tools can be applied to improve relationships at work. The Technology Rubric can help to explain new platforms, guide purchase decisions, and improve the quality of training. The Conversation Map can lead interactions away from tension and distrust and toward a spirit of mutual productivity. And The Workflow Distributor can help you decide who is best suited to tackle every task you have—and how to engage them in taking on that challenge.

Now is the time to change the conversation. Today is your opportunity to improve and renew your workplace relationships.

Let's build bridges across ages.

Addendum: Time Marches On

In 2013 when this book was first published, the Millennials (born between 1980 and 2000) were well into the workforce and the subject of considerable discussion.

But in 2019, the next generation is starting to take jobs, create companies, and influence the world. Whether you call them the Generation Z, The Centennials, post-Millenials or the Homeland Generation, this cohort is rising. They are here and already are having an impact.

But as with any new generation, even defining the range is challenging. Some experts believe the previous generation should be shortened to end in the mid-1990s. Others feel we do not have enough information yet to characterize this group.

Still, patterns have emerged. The Homeland Generation is the first to be born with no memory of the terrorist attacks of September 11, and for whom the 2008 election of President Barack Obama may be their most formative national event. It is also a generation born into an economic recession, and one faced with the highest student debt and the smallest increase in income opportunity for their age.

But what these youngsters are most known for is technology. They have never known a world without smartphones and tablets, and have been thinking about online privacy since they made their first accounts. This is a generation which sociologist Anthony Turner describes as having "a digital bond to the Internet" and who use social networks to escape from emotional and mental struggles they experience offline.

Individuals in this generation identify themselves as who they are online as much—if not more—than they do in the so-called real world. Indeed for the post-Millenials Generation, cyberspace is just as legitimate and important as their physical space.

As for their objectives, the central premise remains: **The agenda of every generation is to pursue their own ideas.** Every generation insists its dreams are important and relevant.

But for Generation Z, those dreams may be even more challenging to their predecessors than ever before. Initial surveys indicate that young people have extremely liberal views on political topics like gender and social justice. A poll published in January 2019 by Axios reported that 61% of the Homeland Generation responded positively to the word "socialism"—the only age group supporting that term more than "capitalism."

It's hard to know how best to interact with this generation in the workforce, especially since it's just starting to happen. But one thing remains clear: their entrance is undeniable. By the year 2030, over 60 million young people will come of age.

And as with every group in modern history, they will change the world forever.

No matter when you were born or what views you bring to the work you do, chances are you'll be working alongside people who are younger or older than you. And with Generation Z, the potential gap is getting bigger every day.

Even with these differences, listening, learning and understanding continue to be the best way to build bridges across the ages. And if you're willing to be open to what they have to say, perhaps they too will be ready to listen to you.

When you get back to work, look around for the freshest faces. Those individuals will be leading our companies, our organizations, and our governments someday.

But for now, the present is what matters. Let's work with everyone from every generation to make the present the best it can be.

Robby Slaughter
Indianapolis, Indiana

www.ingramcontent.com/pod-product-compliance
Lightning Source LLC
Chambersburg PA
CBHW021419210526
45463CB00001B/448